VOLUME 13

STORY and ART BY
WOO

HAMBURG // LONDON // LOS ANGELES // TOKYO

Rebirth Vol. 13
created by Woo

Translation - Jennifer Hahm
English Adaptation - Bryce P. Coleman
Associate Editor - Aaron Sparrow
Copy Editor - Suzanne Waldman
Retouch and Lettering - Caren McCaleb
Production Artist - James Lee
Cover Design - Jorge Negrete

Editor - Bryce P. Coleman
Digital Imaging Manager - Chris Buford
Pre-Press Manager - Antonio DePietro
Production Managers - Jennifer Miller and Mutsumi Miyazaki
Art Director - Matt Alford
Managing Editor - Jill Freshney
VP of Production - Ron Klamert
Editor-In-Chief - Mike Kiley
President and C.O.O. - John Parker
Publisher and C.E.O. - Stuart Levy

A **TOKYOPOP**® Manga

TOKYOPOP Inc.
5900 Wilshire Blvd. Suite 2000
Los Angeles, CA 90036

E-mail: info@TOKYOPOP.com
Come visit us online at www.TOKYOPOP.com

ISBN: 1-59532-028-8
First TOKYOPOP printing: April 2005
10 9 8 7 6 5 4 3 2 1
Printed in the USA

STORY THUS FAR

More than 300 years ago, two lost souls were inextricably intertwined. Deshwitat L. Rudbich, a vampire, and Kalutika Maybus, an aristocrat. They would become the unlikeliest of friends, and later, the fiercest of allies. But a cruel fate, orchestrated by an unknown force beyond time itself, was to tear their friendship—their very worlds—apart. Today they are mortal enemies, locked in a struggle of apocalyptic proportions. Deshwitat, joined by an immortal comrade from his past and a rag-tag group of stalwarts, seeks his revenge upon Kalutika for the murder of his beloved Lilith all those centuries ago.

Kalutika, now a god-like being, plots his own revenge. One of unholy retribution against all of mankind for years of cruelty heaped upon him as a human.

But before their paths can cross again, Deshwitat must gain abilities that will enable him to challenge Kalutika's near-limitless power. It is a quest that has brought him to a far-off land, full of strange people and customs... New York City.

REBIRTH

Vol 13

Chapter 50:
Lord of the Vampires

New York City,
U.S.A.

빵—
빵… 빵
WHOA.
뚜벅
뚜벅

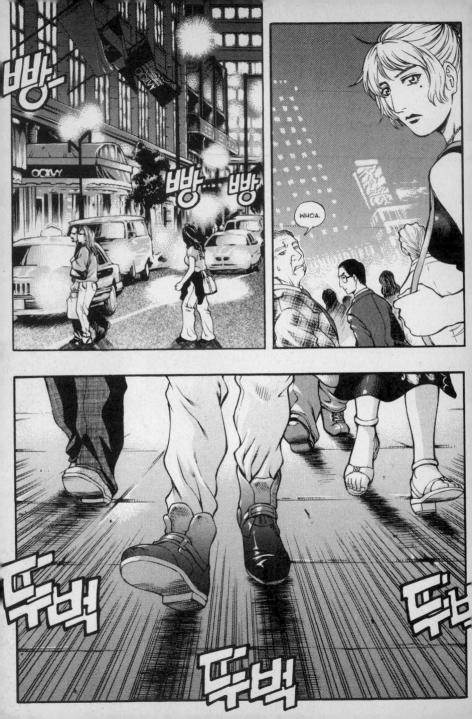

B2
TAKE OUT!
THIS WAY. QUICKLY NOW.
UT
9:00
멈칫
끼익
움찔-
WHAT'S WRONG, DESH?
HUNH?
NOTHING... KEEP MOVING.

HA! I LOVE THIS CITY! WOMEN EVERYWHERE!
I COULDN'T AGREE MORE, MASTER!
STAY DOWN!
ARE THEY GONE?
I...I THINK SO...
TH-THAT WAS CLOSE. WE ALMOST GOT CAUGHT!
I KNOW.
WE NEED TO BE MORE CAREFUL. IF DESH SEES US...

ANYWAY... THANKS FOR COMING WITH ME, REMI.
I DON'T THINK I COULD HAVE DONE THIS BY MYSELF.
THAT'S OKAY. THERE'S NOTHING BACK IN KOREA FOR ME ANYWAY.
AND I DON'T INTEND TO JUST SIT QUIETLY AND WAIT FOR THE END OF THE WORLD, EITHER.
BUT TELL ME, MILL. WHY WERE YOU SO EAGER TO FOLLOW THEM?
HUH? WHAT DO YOU MEAN?
WELLLL... IS IT MAYBE BECAUSE YOU WANT TO STAY CLOSE TO DESH?
AH! MILLENEAR! WATCH OUT!!
OH! SORRY!

끼이이익~!
CRAP!
I WAS JOKING, OKAY?! DON'T TRY AND KILL US! SHEESH!
HUFF HUFF
HA HA! DON'T WORRY, MILL. I WON'T TELL--
UH, NO, REMI...IT'S NOT THAT... IT'S JUST THAT, WELL... I...
HEY!
WH- WHERE'D THEY ALL GO?!
OH, NO! WE'VE LOST THEM!
휘이잉~

'SCUSE ME, MISS.

EH?

YOU TWO GALS MILLENEAR AND REMI?

아이앙!

YES. BUT HOW DID YOU--?

HERE. S'FUR YOU.

슥

WHAT IS IT?

COULDN'T SAY. A SECOND AGO, A GIGANTIC BLOND-HAIRED FELLA WITH A SCARRED FACE HANDS ME $50. TOLD ME TO GIVE YA' THIS.

HE DIDN'T SAY NO MORE.

GIGANTIC MAN...

BLOND HAIR...

SCARRED FACE. THAT'S...

YEAH, IT'S RETT!!

OH, MY!

LET'S SEE WHAT IT IS.

흐이익

KNOWING RETT, IT'S PROBABLY PORN.

Communication Parchment: Acts much like a mystical cell phone and homing device.

THANKS, GRANPA! YOU SAVED OUR LIVES!
DON'T THANK ME, I GOT PAID.
THANK YOU, RETT...
RIGHT!
WELL?! TAKE A LOOK! LET'S FIND THEM!
...I THINK THEY'RE... UNDER-GROUND?
HMM... ALL RIGHT, THEY'RE HEADING NORTH...
THEY'RE STILL VERY CLOSE.
AND IF I'M READING THIS RIGHT...

WELL, IT'S NOT EXACTLY RUSH HOUR DOWN HERE, NOW IS IT?
뚜벅
뚜벅
THIS SUBWAY ROUTE HAS BEEN LONG SINCE ABANDONED, MASTER.
뚜벅
A FACT THAT BEGS THE QUESTION...
WHERE THE HELL ARE YOU TAKING US?
TO OUR SECT'S NEW YORK BASE OF OPERATIONS, BROTHER DESH. AS YOU WELL KNOW.
61
WE ARE ALMOST THERE.
ARGH! I'M NOT YOUR BROTHER!

MORE THAN ANYTHING, IT'S REALLY AN INFORMATION GATHERING AND PROCESSING CENTER FOR THE NINJA SECT.

IT IS ALSO AFFILIATED WITH OUR KUNOICHI SISTERS.

Kunoichi = Female ninja

TELL ME MORE, LITTLE BROTHER!

AH, WE'RE HERE.

A BIT OSTENTATIOUS FOR A SECRET BASE, EH?

AS DEADLY AS THEY ARE BEAUTIFUL, MASTER.

NEVER JUDGE A NINJA BY THEIR COVER...

井本
山本
中山
木村
川村
山田
野口
井上
金木
天野
岩村
二岡
清水
宮本

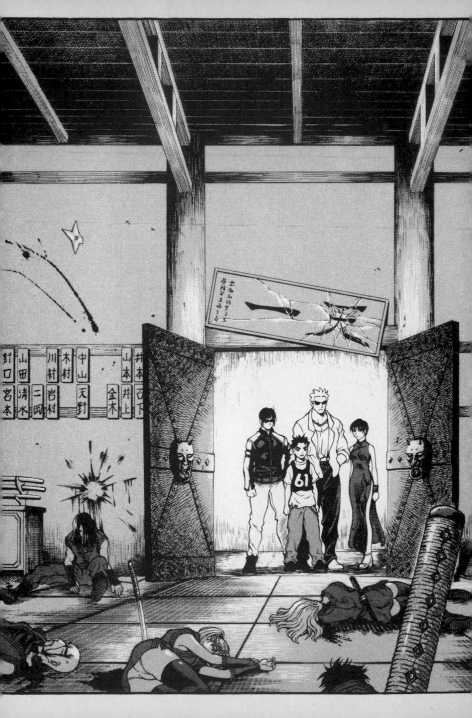

天下一

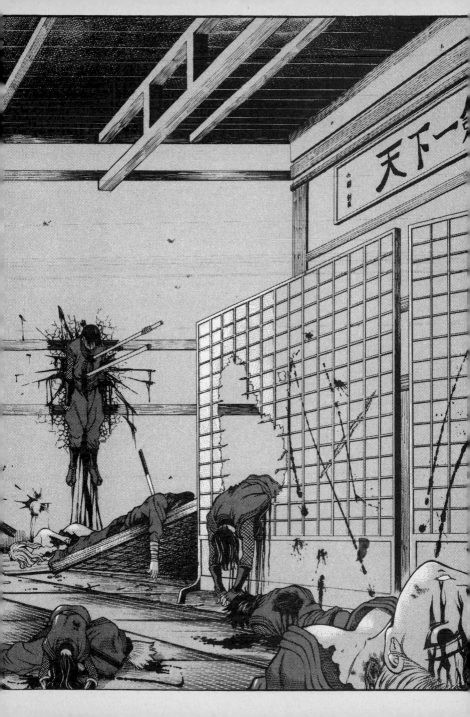

OKAAAY...
THIS IS HARSH.
THERE WERE THREE OR FOUR ATTACKERS.
THIS WAS NO IN-AND-OUT CLEAN HIT.
WHOEVER DID THIS...
...REALLY ENJOYED THEIR WORK.
HATE TO SAY IT...
...BUT IT LOOKS LIKE--
IT WAS VAMPIRES.
VAMPIRES... LIKE ME.

OOH... OH...
SISKA!! YOU ARE ALIVE!!
EI... EIJI...?
VA- VAMPIRES... CAME IN...
SO MUCH BLOOD...
BLOOD...
GET BACK!
DON'T GET SO CLOSE!
TOO FAST...
BLOOD...
EIJI, I SAID...
...GET BACK!
THEY WANTED...
BLOOD...
I WANT...

JUST ONE BITE...
...YOUR SWEET...
...SWEET BLOOD!

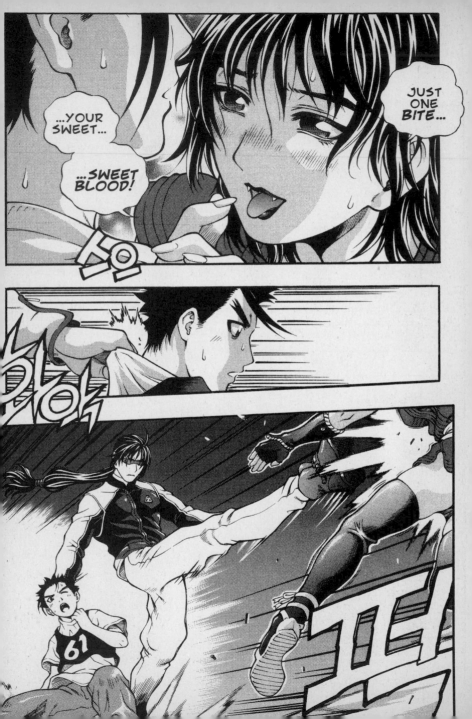

피아ㅇ

AAH...
AAH...
AAH...

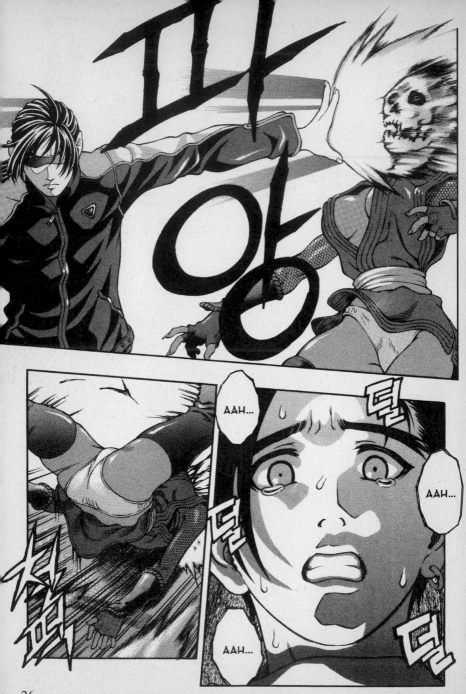

OH, AND FOR SOME REASON TWO OF THEM ARE ACTING SEPARATELY.
THEY SEEM TO BE TAILING THE OTHERS.
OF COURSE.
AS YOU COMMAND...
...MY MASTER, MR. GREY.
LORD OF THE VAMPIRES!

CHAPTER 51:
SAND OF THE DEAD

XBOX
TAXI
TAXI
HOTEL
LIBERTY

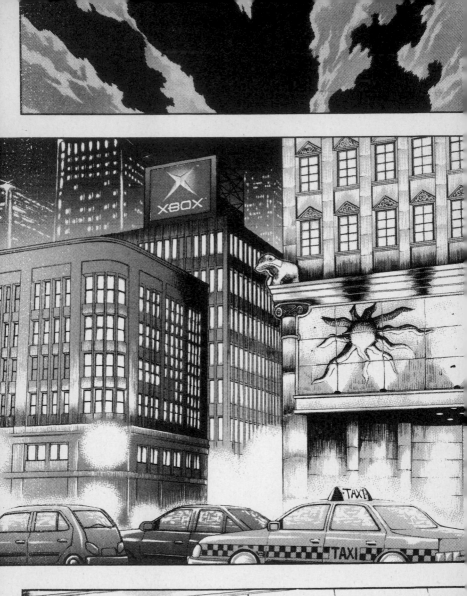

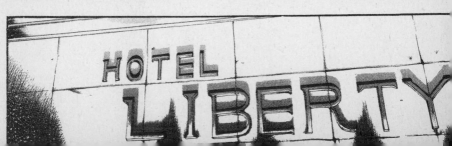

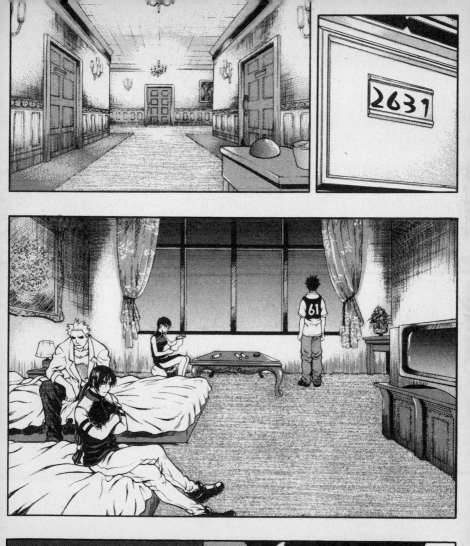

KILL THEM ALL!!
GOOD CHOICE.
DON'T LET THEM SUFFER FOR ETERNITY...
NOT LIKE THIS!
武
PLEASE... JUST KILL THEM.

NEED HELP, DESH?
I THINK I CAN MANAGE.
I'M SORRY...
I'M SORRY... MY FRIENDS!

Hssss!!

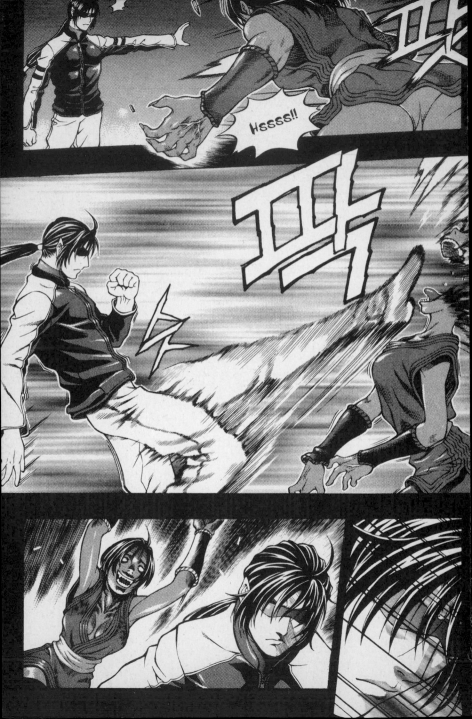

HURK?!

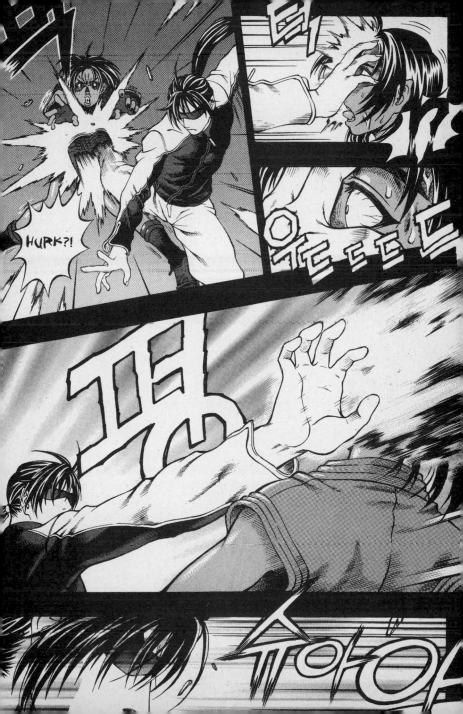

SKREEE!!
AHK!
GAH!
HSSS!!
THUD!

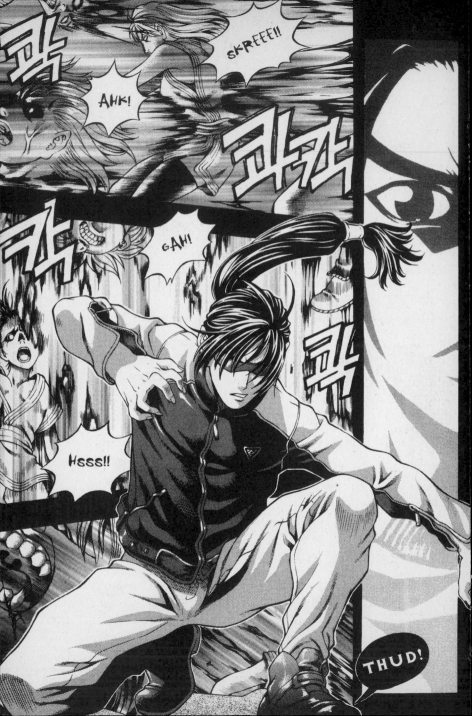

I'M SORRY...
DAMMIT!
DON'T BEAT YOURSELF UP, EIJI. YOU DID THE RIGHT THING.
AND WHEN WE FIND THE BLOODSUCKERS THAT DID YOUR FRIENDS...
...WE'LL GET SOME PAYBACK-- BIG-TIME.
THAT WE WILL, MASTER RETT.
AND... THANK YOU.

ANYTHING YET, BERYUN?
ANY CLUES IN THOSE DOCUMENTS WE BROUGHT FROM THE NINJAS' BASE?
NO, I'M AFRAID NOT.
MOST OF THE DOCUMENTS WERE COMPLETELY DESTROYED. AND THE ONE FRAGMENT LEFT...
...SEEMS ALL BUT MEANING-LESS.
THESE PARCHMENTS WEREN'T SIMPLY COLLATERAL DAMAGE.
I BELIEVE THEY WERE DESTROYED INTENTIONALLY.
HMPH. SOMETHING WE WEREN'T SUPPOSED TO SEE, I GUESS.
Marlboro
EIJI... GOT ANY IDEAS?
NONE. HEADQUARTERS IN JAPAN INSTRUCTED ME TO BRING YOUR TEAM HERE.
ONCE HERE, THE NEW YORK GROUP WOULD KNOW THE NEXT STEP, BUT NOW...

THIS IS MADDENING!

WE'VE COME ALL THIS WAY TO A DEAD END?!

I'LL REPORT TO MASTER TAE.

Communication Parchment↑

WHY BOTHER? SHE'S THE ONE WHO SENT US ON THIS WILD GOOSE CHASE TO BEGIN WITH!

ANCIENT SCROLLS... THE STARS... BAH! I DON'T THINK THE OLD WOMAN'S ALL THERE!

AND YET... VAMPIRES! VAMPIRES STILL EXIST IN THE WORLD?

OTHER THAN MY FATHER, I'VE NEVER KNOWN A PURE VAMPIRE BEFORE.

EH?

ROOM SERVICE...

THERE'S A PACKAGE FOR MR. RUDBICH.

ANYONE EXPECTING A PACKAGE...?

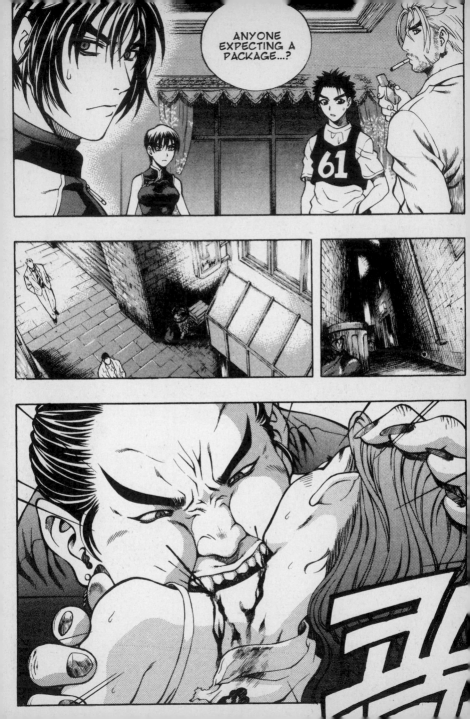

SLURP!

BURP!

GL-GULP!

SCHLUP!

YOU'RE MAKING A PIG OF YOURSELF, LESTER.

YOU NEVER KNOW WHEN TO STOP.

AW...NOW DON'T BE LIKE THAT, RANG.

I'VE WAITED 60 YEARS TO TASTE THESE CITY GIRLS.

JUST CLEAN UP AFTER YOURSELF. WE DON'T NEED THEM SHAMBLING ABOUT.

BELOSE, WHAT ARE THEY UP TO NOW?
The room is bugged.
WHOLE LOTTA NOTHING, AT THE MOMENT, RANG.
TALKIN' 'BOUT SOME PACKAGE THEY JUST GOT.
A PACKAGE?
CAN'T BE NUTHIN' IMPORTANT. 'SIDES...WE TOOK CARE OF ALL THEM NINJAS.
AND MR. GREY TOOK CARE OF THEM OTHERS. SO AIN'T NO ONE GONNA TELL RUDBICH NOTHIN'.
HMM... PERHAPS.
PERHAPS IT IS NOTHING...

BELOSE!!
WHAT'S INSIDE THAT BOX?!
WHA--?!
IT AIN'T NOTHIN'! I WOULDA TOLD YOU IF IT WAS SOMETHIN' FISHY!
SOME-THING...
...FEELS STRANGE...
IT'S LIKE...
IT'S LIKE...
DAMMIT!
WE NEED TO GET THAT BOX.
HUH?
LET IT GO, RANG. YOU KNOW WHAT MR. GREY SAID... SURVEILLANCE ONLY.
THERE'S NO WAY WE CAN TAKE THAT GUY ON. GREY TOLD US TO STAY IN PLACE OR WE'D BE DEAD.
I KNOW.
BUT I THINK IF WE STAY HERE... WE'LL LOSE THEM.

BESIDES...
...MAYBE WE CAN'T TAKE HIM ON DIRECTLY...
...BUT STEALING A LITTLE BOX ISN'T OUT OF BOUNDS, IS IT?
WOO HOO! YUR ONE GUTSY GAL, RANG!
AND YUR TAKIN' FULL RESPONSIBILITY!
YOU GOT IT.
YEAH! LET'S GO!
HOTEL DELGADO
WELL... WHAT ARE THEY DOING?

UM... THEY'RE JUST TALKING. THAT'S IT!
MAYBE THEY'RE JUST GOING TO STAY HERE TONIGHT?
ARGH! WHAT ARE THEY SAYING? THIS IS SO FRUSTRA-TING!
TSK...THAT BIG JERK!
IF RETT DOESN'T TURN ON THE SOUND OF THE PARCHMENT, THERE'S NOTHING WE CAN DO.
HE GAVE US THE DARN THING...WHY WON'T HE LET US HEAR?!

YAAAWN!
LET'S GET SOME SLEEP. TOMORROW WILL BE A LONG DAY.
'KAY!
HM...?
REMI, LET ME HAVE THE BINOCULARS FOR A MOMENT.
HERE...
INTERESTING...
WHAT?

INTERESTING...
WHAT KIND OF PLAY IS THIS? EMPTY BOX, ANONYMOUS SENDER...?
THIS IS NO SIMPLE, EMPTY BOX. THERE IS SOMETHING MORE.
I AGREE. THERE'S SOME SORT OF ENERGY EMANATING FROM IT.
DOESN'T LOOK SO SPECIAL.
SHOULD I SMASH IT?

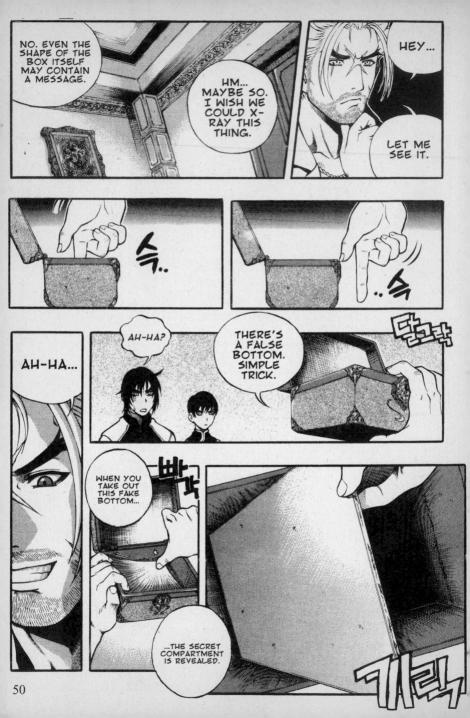

NO. EVEN THE SHAPE OF THE BOX ITSELF MAY CONTAIN A MESSAGE.

HM... MAYBE SO. I WISH WE COULD X-RAY THIS THING.

HEY...

LET ME SEE IT.

슥..

..슥

AH-HA?

THERE'S A FALSE BOTTOM. SIMPLE TRICK.

AH-HA...

WHEN YOU TAKE OUT THIS FAKE BOTTOM...

...THE SECRET COMPARTMENT IS REVEALED.

IT'S...
THIS IS A...
IT'S A VA-VAMPIRE'S...
...SAND OF THE DEAD!
SO THAT IS THE ENERGY I WAS SENSING.
UH... EXCUSE ME, BUT WHAT IS "SAND OF THE DEAD"?
IN THIS CASE, IT'S THE DISTILLED ESSENCE OF A VAMPIRE.
ONLY THE BLOOD OF A VIRGIN WILL REGENERATE THE CREATURE.

WHAT'S THE CALL, DESH? THIS VAMP COULD BE ANYBODY, WE CAN'T JUST--
RETT, WE HAVE NO CHOICE. WE REANIMATE IT.
WE'RE STUMBLING BLINDLY HERE. THIS MAY BE OUR ONLY CLUE.
GOOD POINT. BERYUN, BE A GOOD GIRL AND GIVE US A DROP OF BLOOD.
I'M SORRY, RETT...
...BUT IT WOULD BE IMPOSSIBLE WITH MY BLOOD.
OH, REALLY?
BUT IF YOU'RE...

WH-WHAT DO YOU MEAN, "IMPOSSIBLE" ?!
HEE!
YOU MEAN TO TELL ME THAT YOU...?!
HOW COULD YOU?!
IT'S ALWAYS THE QUIET ONES, ISN'T IT?!
UH... RETT?
WH-WHY NOT ME?! WHY?!
TEMPTRESS!
OOH!
BLOODY TEMPT--!
OOH!
IDIOT.

OOOOH...
SO, BERYUN...
...YOU'RE SAYING THAT YOUR BLOOD WON'T WORK BECAUSE YOU AREN'T HUMAN?
YES.
발딱
UH... RIGHT. I KNEW THAT.
DAMN... THEN IT WILL HAVE TO WAIT.
WHOSE BLOOD REVIVED YOU, BROTHER DESH?
REMI'S. AND DON'T CALL ME BROTHER.
OKAY, OKAAAY...
ARGH! THE ONE THING THAT BIRD-BRAIN IS GOOD FOR...
I NEVER DREAMED I'D WISH THOSE TWO WERE STILL WITH US!
HEY...NO ONE TO BLAME BUT YOURSELF, DESH.

OH WELL, WE'LL JUST HAVE TO FIND ONE.
A VIRGIN? IN NEW YORK THESE DAYS?
WHAT, ARE YOU GONNA ASK EVERY GIRL, "ARE YOU A VIRGIN"?
ANY BETTER IDEAS?!
HERE'S THE SEARCH CRITERIA!
1) THE UGLIEST!
2) THE FATTEST!
3) THE TACKIEST! IF WE LIMIT OUR SEARCH TO THESE GIRLS, WE'LL SAVE SOME TIME.
A BRILLIANT ANALYSIS THAT CRUELLY GETS TO THE HEART OF THE MATTER, BUT...
...I SHUDDER TO THINK OF THE SELECTION PROCESS THAT LIES AHEAD.
WANTED
H-HOW RIGHT YOU ARE, MASTER.
WILL YOU TWO SHUT UP AND--

LOOK OUT!

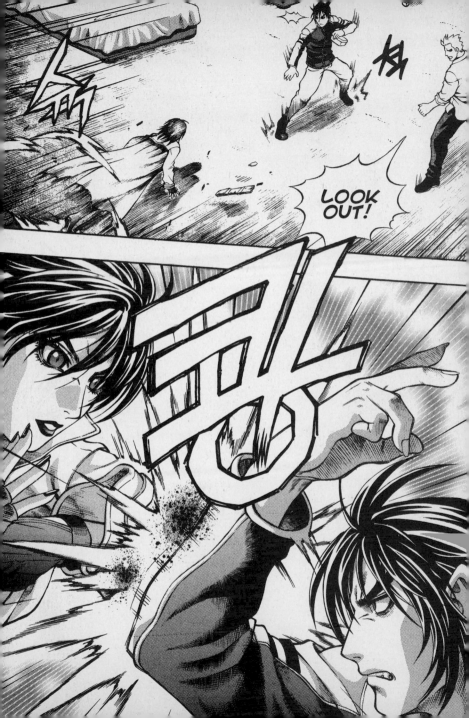

A VAMPIRE!
HEH HEH
?

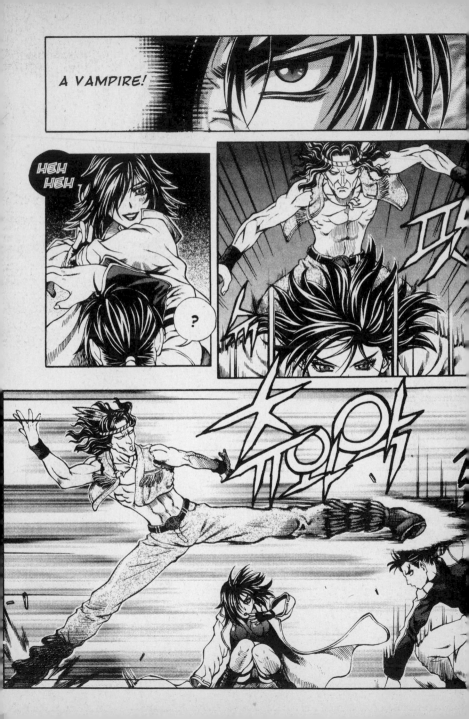

HRAH!
HOLD THIS, BOY!
OH! R-RIGHT!
TARGET LOCATED.
MOVE IT, RANG!! DON'T GIVE 'EM NO ROOM!
GOT IT!

BATTLE SWORD!
OHM!

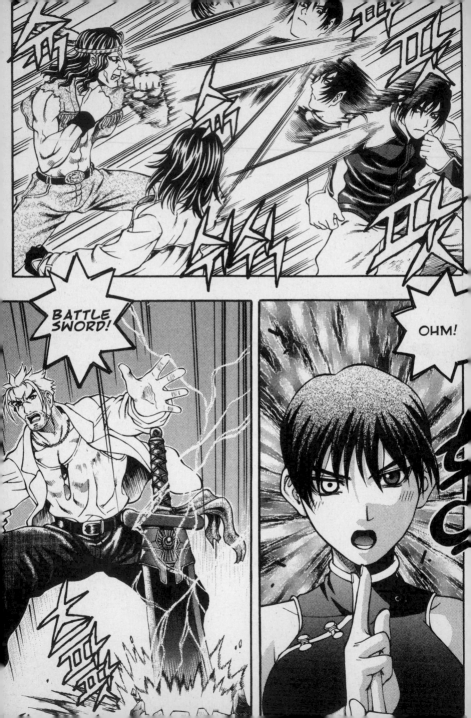

TOO CRAMPED. WE NEED TO SEPARATE THEM.
RIGHT.
EH...?!
ACK!!
BELOSE...!
EEK!
탁

AAAH!!
KA-KAFF!

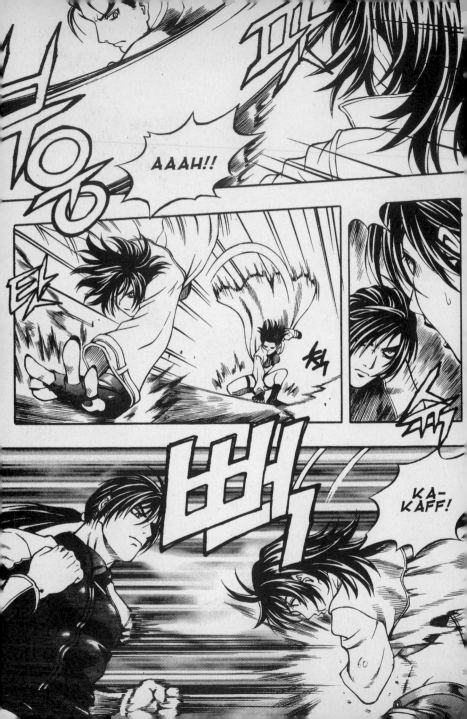

RANG!!
GREY WAS RIGHT! THESE GUYS ARE OUTTA OUR LEAGUE!
SHH! WE NEED THAT BOX! DON'T SHOW ANY WEAKNESS NOW!
NOW, THEN. WHO ARE YOU?
AND WHAT DO YOU WANT?
I'M RANG. HE'S BELOSE.
WE'RE UNDER ORDERS TO TAKE YOU OUT.
"TAKE US OUT"?
SHE'S PUTTING ON A BRAVE FACE, BUT...
...HER LEGS SHAKE LIKE A NEWBORN CALF'S.

SHE'S LYING, DESH. THEY WEREN'T TRYING TO KILL US.
THEY'RE AFTER SOMETHING.
MY THOUGHTS EXACTLY, RETT.
A-HA...
멀뚱~
SHE'S HOT!
DAMN, I SHOULD GET IN THERE...
THEY WERE QUITE TASTY...
THE NINJAS, I MEAN.
BUT THEY WERE WEAK AND AFRAID.
AND THEY DIED...IN AGONY.

IT WAS YOU!!
Y-YOU...
YOU FOOL! GET BACK!
THEY WANT THE BOX!
THE BOX?!
GOT IT!
UH?!

LESTER! TAKE IT! GO! GO!
WHA-? ANOTHER ONE?!
HEH HEH... LESTER MAY BE FAT, BUT HE'S FAST.
AN' A HEAD START'S ALL HE NEEDS.
滅鬼
JUK NAH JUK GA OHM!
YE HE HE!
!

AWW... CRAP.
RANG! I GOTTA PROBLEM...
SA BA HA!
BE-BELOOOSE!
KYAK!!

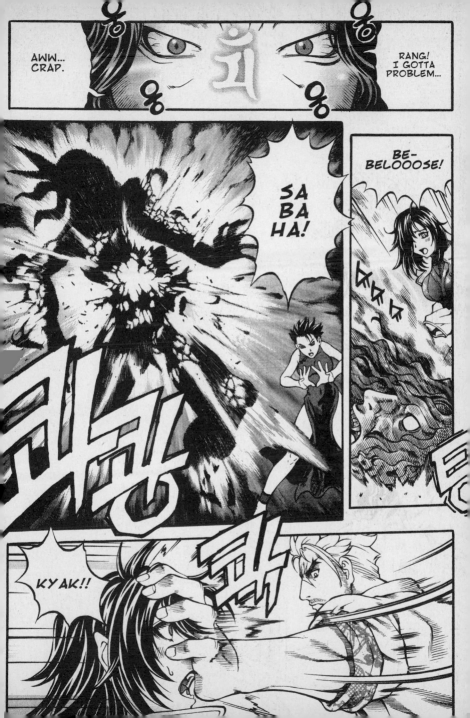

DON'T KILL HER, RETT!! SHE HAS INFORMATION!
I'LL GET THE OTHER ONE!
MMPH!!
RIGHT, DESH!
HRGH!
THE FAT ONE'S SPEED IS INCREDIBLE!
HA! COME AND GET ME!
HOLY-

-SPEAR!!
MILLENEAR?!

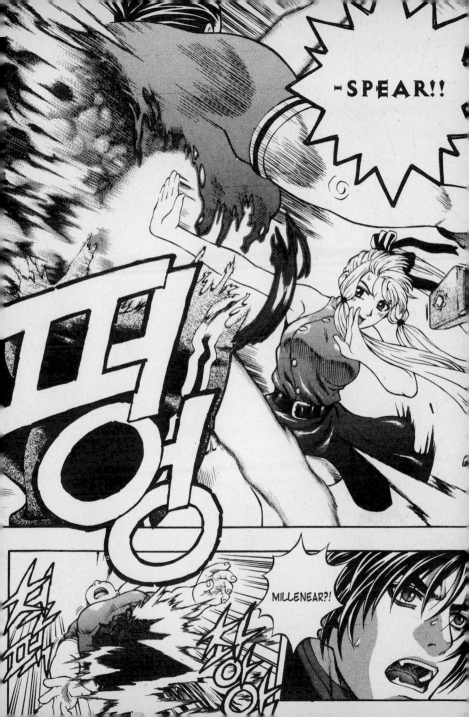

YOU WERE ABOUT TO LOSE HIM, DESHWITAT.
HOW EMBARRASSING WOULD THAT HAVE BEEN?
A "THANK YOU" WOULD BE NICE...
DUH...
BEHIND YOU!
LOOK OUT!
REMI, CATCH!
AH! I-I GOT IT!

MILLENEAR!
SHE'S GONE!
MILLE-- SHE'S...
U... URK...
H-HEY... KOFF! HEY, BIG F-FELLA...
HUH? YOU STILL KICKING?
Y-YOU EVER-KOFF! YOU EVER HEAR A SOMETHIN' CALLED...
...A PYRRHIC VICTORY?
CLICK!

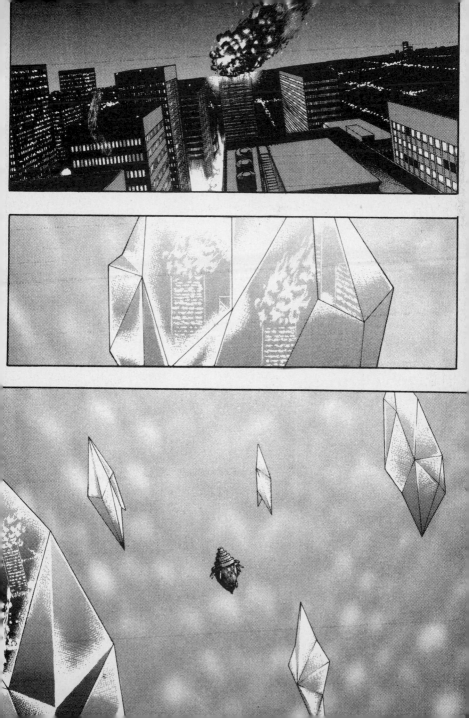

AND NOW...
...COUNCIL ITEM 7418. PRESENT YOURSELF, KALUTIKA.

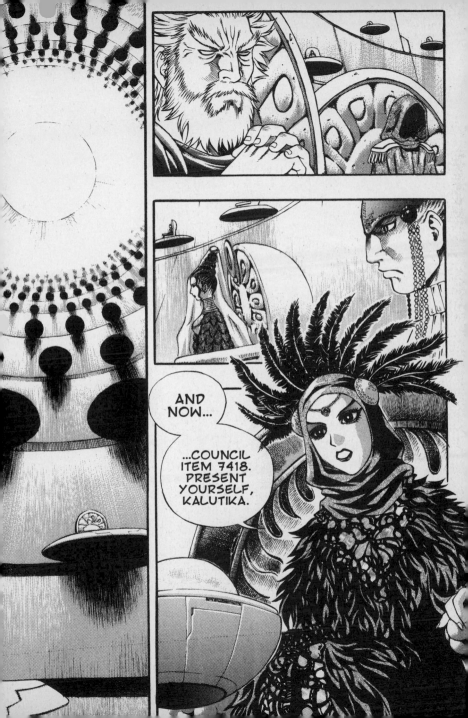

CHAPTER 52:
THE FIRST CLUE

IT IS AN EXERCISE IN FUTILITY.
YOU ARE A YOUNG GOD, KALUTIKA.
AND A FOOLISH ONE.
DURING YOUR ENTIRE TENURE AS THE GOD OF LIGHT, RULING OVER THE KINGDOM OF EARTH...
...HOW MANY TIMES HAVE YOU BROUGHT THIS EXACT REQUEST BEFORE THE COUNCIL?

YOUR EXCELLENCY...
THIS WILL BE THE 179TH.
AMELUS, GODDESS OF WISDOM, I BEG YOUR INDULGENCE.
179. DO YOU KNOW THE SIGNIFICANCE OF THIS NUMBER?
OVER THESE HUNDREDS OF YEARS, I HAVE PRESIDED OVER EXACTLY 179 SESSIONS. AND EACH TIME, YOU HAVE MADE THIS REQUEST.
WHEN WILL YOU ACCEPT OUR DENIAL?

LORD AMELUS...
...IF YOU WOULD BUT EXAMINE MY CASE--
HEAR ME WELL, KALUTIKA.
YOU MAY CONTINUE TO MAKE THIS UNFOUNDED REQUEST...
...THIS REQUEST TO DESTROY THE KINGDOM OF EARTH...
...UNTIL THE NEXT MILLENNIUM. BUT IT WILL STILL BE REJECTED.
WE ARE NOT THE INSANE GODS OF OLD, KALUTIKA.

SHALL I TAKE THAT...
...AS A "NO," YOUR EXCELLENCY?
IMPUDENT WHELP! SUCH DISRESPECT!
NOVICE! THIS IS WHY HUMANS CANNOT BE GODS!
HE IS GUIDED BY HUMAN EMOTIONS!
SILENCE!
I DEMAND ORDER!
YOUR DESIRE FOR REVENGE...
...TROUBLES ME, LORD KALUTIKA.
YOU ARE A GOD OF LIGHT, NOT DARKNESS.
YOUR PURPOSE IS TO ENLIGHTEN...NOT TO DESTROY.

ARE THEY NOT INTER-CHANGEABLE?
ENLIGHTEN-MENT... DESTRUC-TION...
BESIDES, HUMANITY IS A PESTILENCE AMID THE UNIVERSE...ITS ANNIHILATION WILL LEAD TO THE DAWN OF A NEW AGE.
WHAT?!
YOU ARE A DISGRACE, KALUTIKA!
YOU SHAME THE COUNCIL WITH YOU VILENESS!
A MERE NOVICE GOD SPEAKS TO US THUS?!
YOU HAVE LEFT ME SPEECHLESS, KALUTIKA...

WHA-
WHAT?!
WHAT
ARE YOU
SAYING?
ENTER,
LILITH!

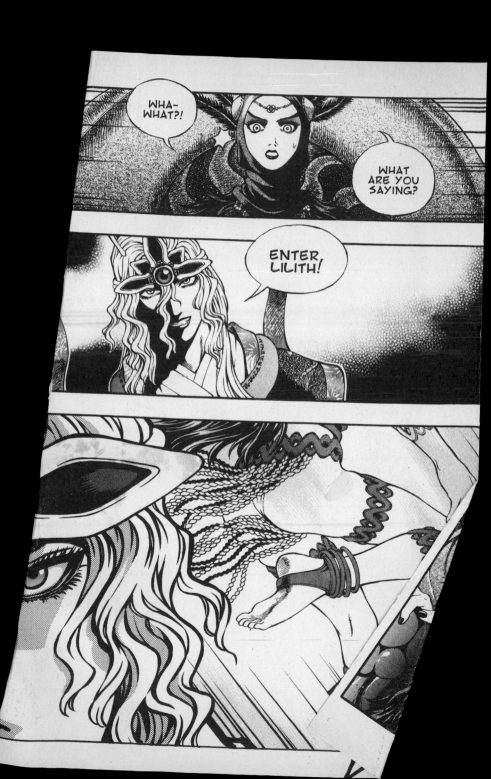

DID YOU KNOW THAT THERE IS NOW A NEW GOD'S SEED ON EARTH?
IF YOU CONTINUE ALONG THIS PATH, WE SHALL HAVE NO CHOICE BUT TO END YOUR RULE AND APPOINT ANOTHER.
NO NEED... I'LL NOT MAKE THE REQUEST AGAIN.
IT'S TOO LATE TO RETRACT YOUR STATEMENTS, KALUTIKA.
RETRACT...? HA HA! I'VE NOT RETRACTED ANYTHING.
I'M SAYING, YOU'LL NEVER AGAI HEAR MY REQUEST...
I'LL NOT DISCUSS THIS FURTHER. LEAVE US NOW AND REPENT. WE WILL DECIDE UPON WHAT ACTIONS WE SHALL TAKE.

IS IT DONE?
IT IS DONE...
BUT I BEG YOU TO RECONSIDER, KALUTIKA.

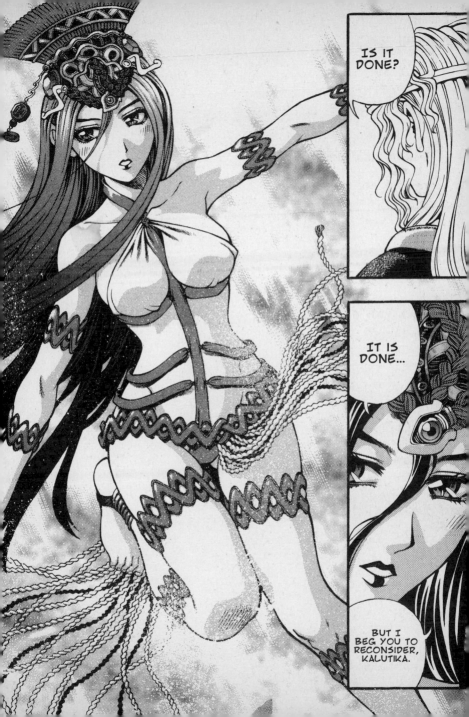

ONLY GODS MAY ENTER HERE! HOW DARE YOU BRING THIS ATTENDANT?!
REMOVE HER!
CHANCELLOR! WE SHOULD NOT WAIT! EXILE KALUTIKA!
LIKE CACKLING HENS.
AND THERE'S A FOX IN THE HENHOUSE.
AH?!

YOU KNOW WHAT THEY SAY...
TOO MANY GODS SPOIL THE PANTHEON!
NO!
AAAH!
AIEEE!!

쾅
HOW CAN THIS BE?! SUCH POWER!
쾅
THIS ENERGY SHOULD NOT EXIST IN OUR DIMENSION!
벌떡
TRUE. BUT I HAVE FRIENDS IN LOW PLACES, EXCELLENCY.
AND THEY...

...HAVE BEEN QUITE ACCOMMO-DATING.
YOU SEE, I'VE MANIPULATED AN INTER-DIMENSIONAL PORTAL.
NO...
IT...C-CAN'T BE...
NOT EVEN YOU...

...WOULD JOIN FORCES WITH...

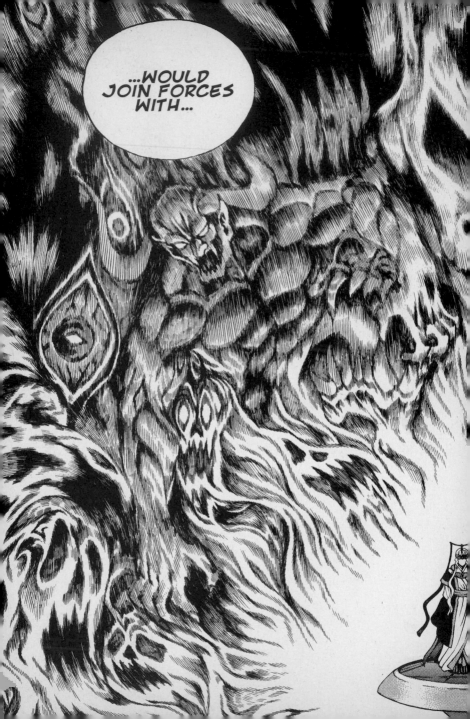

...THE DARK GODS?!

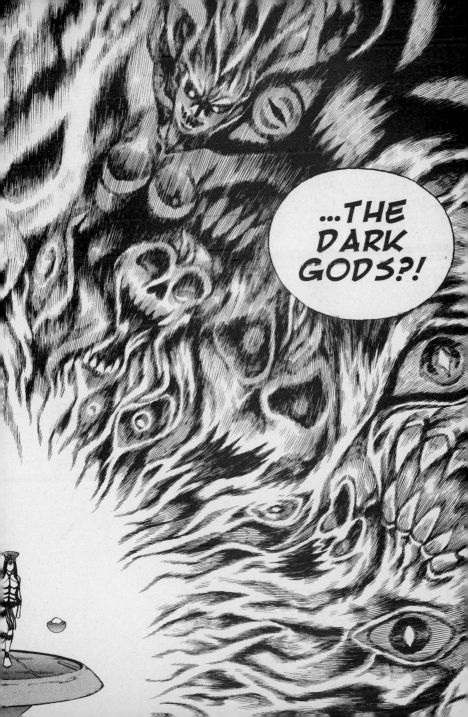

AAAH!
OOF!
IN ORDER TO CONTAIN THE CONFLICTING ENERGIES, THE TEMPLE WILL IMPLODE...
...AND YOU SO-CALLED "GODS" WILL CEASE TO EXIST.
S-SUCH AN ACT WILL...
HUFF
HUFF
...DESTROY YOU AS W-WELL!
HA HA! FEAR NOT, GODDESS OF WISDOM...

DO YOU THINK I WOULD HAVE LEFT MYSELF WITHOUT AN EXIT STRATEGY?
ONCE I CLOSE THE PORTAL BEHIND ME, THESE DARK GODS WILL BE LITTLE MORE THAN LOST CHILDREN.
WHAT IS IT YOU HOPE TO GAIN? POWER?
POWER?
HA! I HAVE ALL I NEED. THAT IS WHAT I PROMISED THESE DEMONS IN EXCHANGE FOR THEIR AID.
I'VE TOLD YOU WHAT I DESIRE... 179 TIMES.
THE TOTAL ANNIHILATION OF HUMANITY... NOTHING MORE!
YOU ARE MAD, KALUTIKA...
MAD!
YES. SO I'VE HEARD.

WHA --? A BOMB?!
DON'T PANIC! GET BEHIND ME!
DARK BARRIER!!

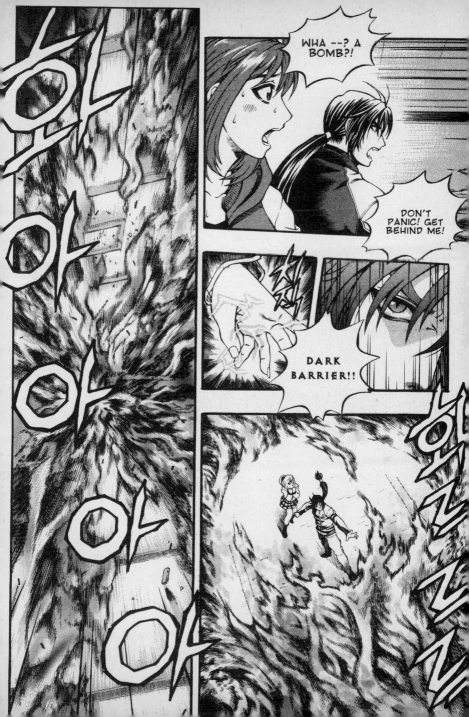

ARSON'S SHIELD!
OH... WOW...!
COOL, BERYUN!
THAT WAS CLOSE!

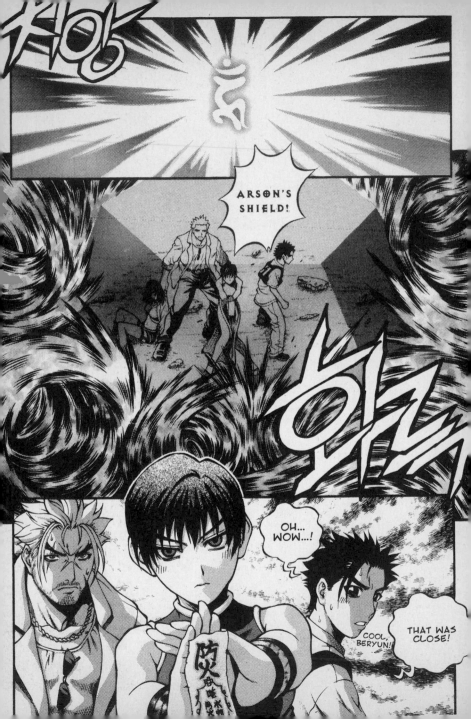

KWANG
AAAH!
RUUUN!

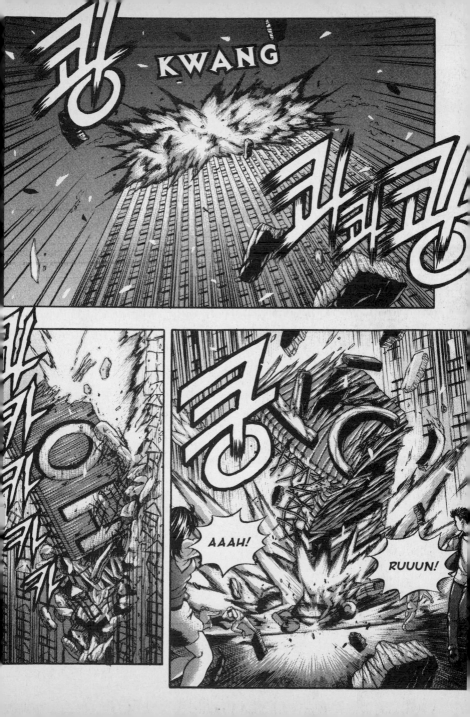

DESH! YOU ALL RIGHT?!
FINE!
REMI?! WHAT ARE YOU DOING HERE?
MILLENEAR...! SHADOW MAN...T-TOOK H-HER...!
OH!
I'LL TELL YOU LATER, RETT. LET'S GET OUT OF HERE!

HURRY! EMERGENCY STAIRS ARE OVER THERE!
RIGHT!

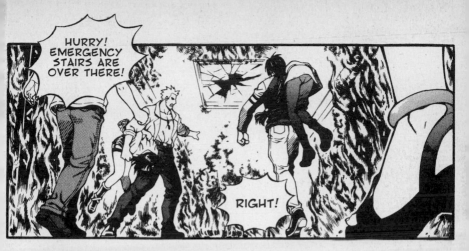

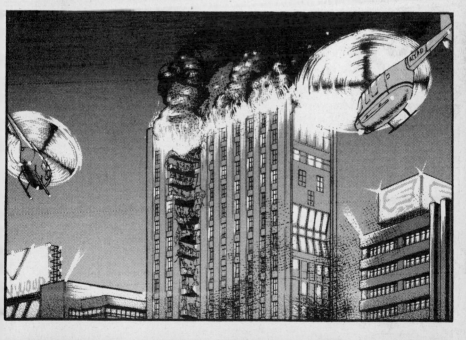

OOOH...

I COULD HAVE DONE WITHOUT COMING BACK HERE...

NO CHOICE, EIJI. WE HAD TO GET DESH INSIDE FAST, BEFORE THE SUN CAME UP.

NOW...WHAT THE HELL WAS REMI GOING ON ABOUT?
WHAT DO YOU MEAN, A "SHADOW MAN" TOOK MILLENEAR?
THAT'S EXACTLY IT. SOMEONE CAME IN AND OUT OF THE SHADOWS SO FAST, I COULDN'T REACT.
WAS HE A VAMPIRE?
I COULDN'T SAY FOR SURE, BUT...
...I THINK SO.
BUT I'M POSITIVE HE'S WITH HER.
HUH?
HEH! YOU'LL GET NOTHING OUT OF ME!

SOB...

SOB...

POOR MILL... WHAT'S GOING TO HAPPEN...?

I DON'T KNOW. BUT WE HAVE TWO CLUES...

THE SAND OF THE DEAD IN THIS BOX...

...AND THE VAMPIRE.

WELL, I SAY WE REVIVE THE SAND FIRST.

BIT RISKY, BUT WHAT THE HELL.

REMI, YOU'RE STILL CHERRY, RIGHT?

WHAT THE HELL?! IT WAS A SIMPLE QUESTION!

ANY EXCUSE TO BE A PERV YOU JERK!

WELL WE NEED TO KNOW, DON'T WE?!

WILL YOU TWO NITWITS SHUT UP?! WE KNOW YOU'RE A VIRGIN--
--SO PUT SOME BLOOD IN THE DAMN BOX!
GULP!
ALL RIGHT... SHEESH!
YOU KNOW...
I'M ACTUALLY A BIT RELIEVED.
SEEING YOU SO WORKED UP...I GUESS THERE'S HOPE FOR MILL AFTER ALL.
JUST GIMME THE BOX.
WHAT DOES THAT MEAN?
GOD YOU'RE THICK, DESH.
OUCH!

HERE WE GO...

OWIE!

OKAAAY... WE'RE WAITING.

REMI, ARE YOU SURE...

WAIT! THE BOX!!

WHAAA?!

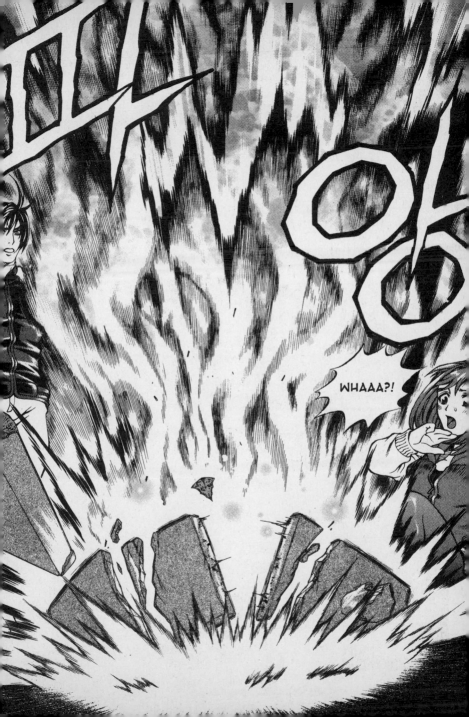

IT'S WORKING...
WHAT IS IT?
STAY CLOSE, PEOPLE! WE MAY HAVE A FIGHT ON OUR HANDS.

トトトト

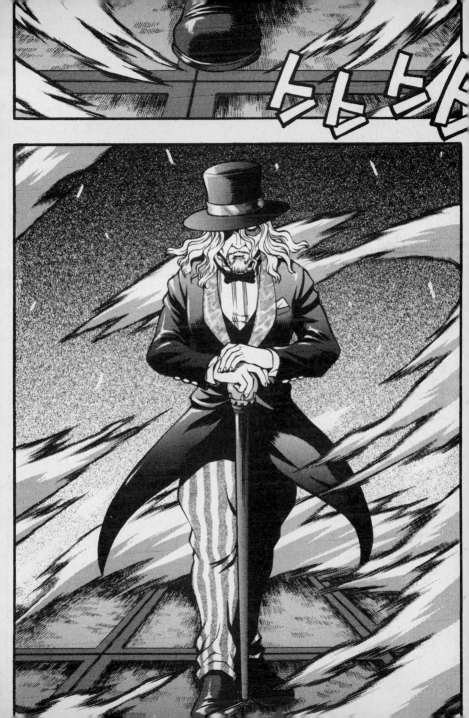

WELL, NOW...
WHAT DO WE HAVE HERE?
AH... DESHWITAT L. RUDBICH, I PRESUME?

CHAPTER 53:
THE TOURNAMENT

HEE HEE...
EASY NOW,
FRIENDS...
EASY.

THIS OLD
MAN IS
NOT YOUR
ENEMY.

ALL RIGHT, SO HE DOESN'T SEEM TO WANT A FIGHT...
HEH HEH HEH HEH...
...BUT WHO IS THIS OLD CODGER, DESH?
WHO, INDEED?
HMPH! WHO IS THIS OLD FOOL?
ALLOW ME TO INTRODUCE MYSELF! FOLKS CALL ME DRAISTAIL...
...AND FOR THE PAST 500 YEARS I HAVE SERVED THE LORD OF THE VAMPIRES.

LORD OF THE...?
A VAMPIRE KING?
HMM...
WOULD THAT BE A MONARCHY, OR AN ELECTED POSITION?
FIRST I'VE HEARD OF SUCH A THING...
YOU MEAN TO SAY YOU'VE NEVER HEARD OF HIM?
PFFT...SEEING AS HOW THAT BASTARD GREY'S KILLED JUST ABOUT EVERYONE...
...I'M NOT SURPRISED.
AH! IS THIS THE PRETTY MISS WHO BROUGHT ME BACK?
WHOA! EASY, OLD-TIMER!
SUCH SPEED!
TSK... SHAME, THOUGH. PRETTY YOUNG FLOWER, AS YET UNPLUCKED.
EEP!
NOT TOO PERSONABLE, THOUGH.
...

FOR THE LOVE OF GOD!
WHY...
...DO I...
...ALWAYS...
HUP!
...ATTRACT THE FREAKIN' PERVERTS!
HM!

SLURP!
SLURP!
SLURP!
EWW!! YOU FREAK!
UHG!
WHAT THE HELL?!
STOP...
STOP...
DON'T ...
NO...
AH...AH, AH, AH...

OOH... DON'T STOP...
UH... CORRECT ME IF I'M WRONG, BUT SHE'S LIKIN' THAT.
AAH...
PHEWWW... I'VE NEVER EVEN HEARD OF THAT TECHNIQUE!
NNGH...
OOOH...
MMM...
AI-YI-YIE...!
HEH HEH... LIKE THAT, GIRLIE?
NEXT TIME I'LL DO IT PROPER!

EH...?
THAT WAS AMAZING! YOU ARE A FREAKIN' SEX-GOD!
LET US SERVE IN YOUR ARMY OF STUDS!
PLEASE, MASTER! TEACH US YOUR TECHNIQUES!
HA HA HA!
PLAY YOUR CARDS RIGHT, BOYS...
...AND I'LL TAKE YOU UNDER MY WING.
WE WILL! WE WILL!
FILL OUR EMPTY HEADS WITH--

NO NEED TO GET TESTY.
PHEW!
I WAS JUST TRYING TO LIGHTEN THE MOOD.
ENOUGH! I'M IN NO MOOD FOR JOKES, OLD MAN.
RIGHT NOW, I WANT ANSWERS!
YES...
HIS EYES... SO COLD...
IT'S LIKE STARING INTO THE VOID...
HEH... WELL, AT LEAST YOUR SPIRIT'S STRONG.
WHAT DOES THAT MEAN?
IT MEANS WHAT IT MEANS.

YOU ARE THE SEED OF CHAOS, DESHWITAT...
A DARK HERO WHO MAY YET SAVE THE WORLD!
HUP.
AN UNHOLY SAVIOR ON THE EVE OF DESTRUCTION.
IT'S A LOFTY POSITION YOU'VE BEEN ELEVATED TO, ISN'T IT?
AND YET...
AND YET...
...COULD YOU EVEN RAISE A FINGER AGAINST KALUTIKA?

OH, PLEASE! COMPARED TO HIM...
...YOU ARE A DOG WHOSE BARK CONCEALS HIS LACK OF TEETH.
OR...
...TO BORROW FREELY FROM A WISE MAN, YOU ARE...

...FULL OF SOUND AND FURY-- SIGNIFYING NOTHING!
HUP!
WHA-?! I COULDN'T EVEN SEE...!
I SPOKE TOO SOON...
...YOU'RE SLOW AS WELL AS WEAK.

I SEE YOU'VE TAKEN A PRISONER.
THEN THE BATTLE WITH GREY HAS BEGUN.
WHAT DOES THIS GREY GUY WANT?
SOMEONE JUST SNATCHED OUR FRIEND, AND I'M GUESSING IT'S HIM.
NOW THAT'S TOO BAD...
I DON'T KNOW WHERE HE IS.
BUT I DO KNOW HE'S THE MOST POWERFUL VAMPIRE I'VE EVER SEEN.
I CHANCED THE SAND OF THE DEAD TO ESCAPE HIM AND CONTACT YOU.
HE DESTROYED ALL OF MY COMRADES...
...IN PURSUIT OF HIS OBJECTIVE.

TO BECOME LORD OF THE VAMPIRES!
AND RULE OVER THE VAMPIRES OF THE EARTH!

BUT...I THOUGHT HE WAS THE VAMPIRE KING?
NOT QUITE. THE CURRENT LORD'S REIGN HAS RECENTLY ENDED.
ACTUALLY... HE WAS ASSASSINATED.
IT HAS NOTHING TO DO WITH US.
SO WHY ATTACK US IF WE'RE NOT INVOLVED?
AH...BUT HE THINKS YOU ARE.
FOR NOW, THE POST IS EMPTY, BUT SOON THE WORLD'S VAMPIRES WILL GATHER TO CHOOSE ANOTHER.
IT'S MY GUESS THAT HE SEES DESHWITAT AS A RIVAL AND WISHES TO ELIMINATE THAT THREAT.
HE SOUNDS LIKE A FOOL! LET HIM PLAY MONARCH IF HE WANTS TO!
I'VE NO INTEREST IN BEING A "VAMPIRE KING"!
JUST LISTEN... YOU MAY CHANGE YOUR MIND.

AHH...YES.
I'VE GOT YOUR ATTENTION NOW.
TELL ME!!
WHAT POWER IS THAT?!
I TOLD YOU, I WAS ONLY GREY'S SUBORDINATE. I DON'T KNOW HIS POWERS...
...OR THE POWERS OF THE VAMPIRE LORD.
BESIDES, I DON'T THINK YOU'RE UP TO THE CHALLENGE.
YOU'VE GOTTEN WEAK.
GRRR...

IF YOU BECAME LORD OF THE VAMPIRES...
...YOU MIGHT GAIN THE POWER TO FACE THE GOD OF LIGHT!

SO TELL ME, POPS...
HOW DO YOU ELECT A VAMPIRE LORD? DRAW STRAWS?
HEH HEH... AN INTERESTING QUESTION, BUTLER.
THE VAMPIRE HIERARCHY HAS EXISTED FOR MILLENNIA.
AS HUMAN SOCIETY FLOURISHED, THE VAMPIRES WERE PUSHED INTO THE SHADOWS.
DURING THE COURSE OF THIS WAR FOR SURVIVAL, MANY REALIZED OUR KIND WOULD NEED A LEADER.
A LEADER TO END THE INTERNAL STRUGGLES AND UNITE US AGAINST THE HUMANS.
THINK OF IT. DO YOU COMPREHEND...
...HOW POWERFUL THAT CREATURE WOULD NEED TO BE?

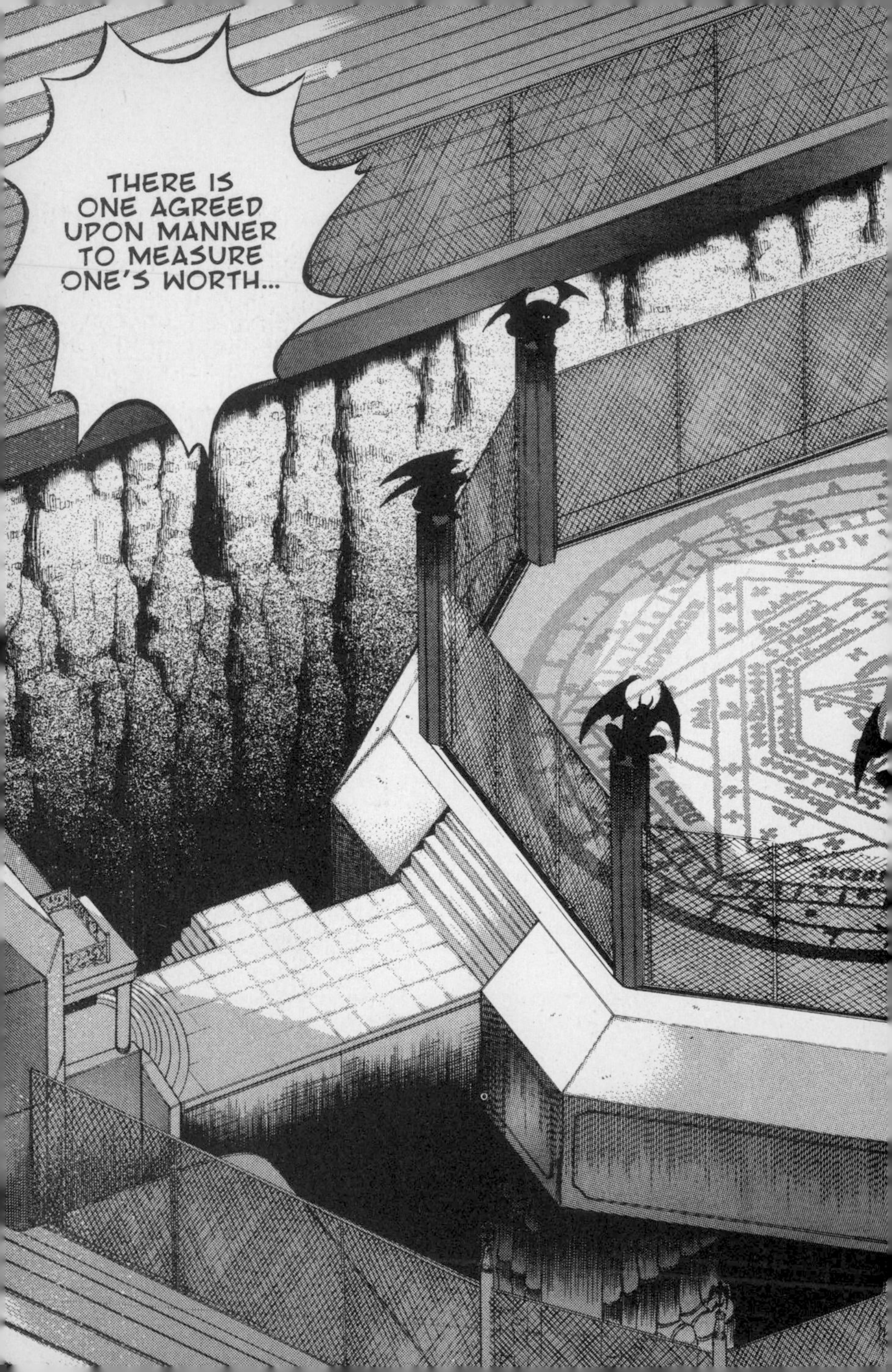
THERE IS ONE AGREED UPON MANNER TO MEASURE ONE'S WORTH...

COUGH!
COUGH!
I AM THE SHROUD. MR. GREY HAS SENT ME.
IT IS BY HIS COMMAND THAT YOU MUST DIE.
THE SH-SHROUD? YOU'RE LYING. N-NEVER HEARD OF YOU!
WHY WOULD MR. GREY WANT ME DEAD?
YOUR IGNORANCE IS NONE OF MY CONCERN.
MY TASK IS YOUR DEATH, NOT YOUR EDIFICATION.

Klod
DIE!!
HEY!
HUH?
NO... MR. GREY!
WHY... WHY...?!

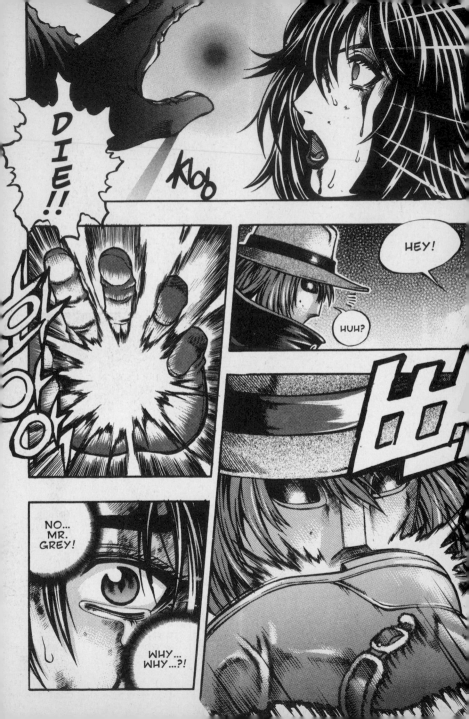

ARGH!!
DESHWITAT!
OUT OF THE FRYING PAN AND INTO THE FIRE, EH?

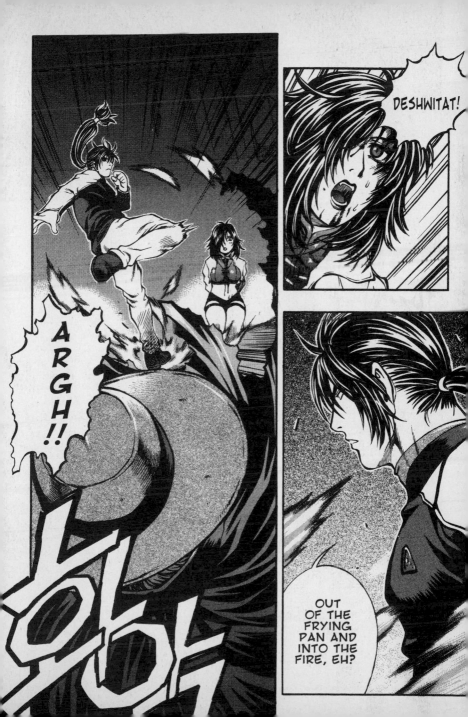

STAY OUT OF THIS!
HURG!!

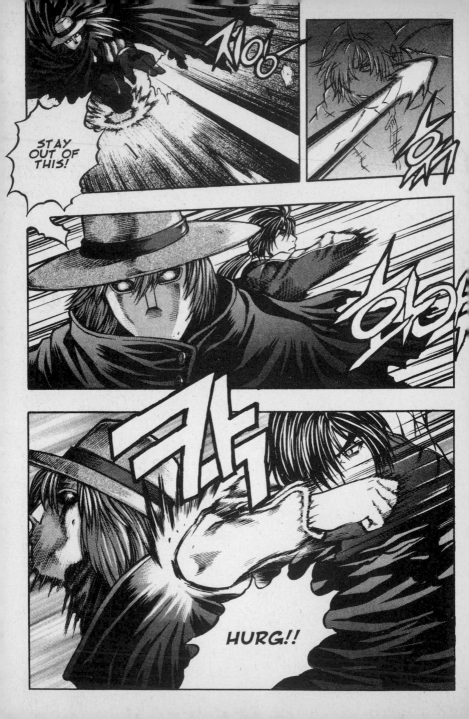

OOF!
AAAHH!
HRRR... IGNORANT FOOL!
I LEAVE YOU NOW, BUT...
...I'LL NOT FORGET THIS INSULT!

COUGH!!
COUGH!!
THE SEAL ON THOSE ROPES...
BERYUN ALSO PUT A TRACING SPELL ON THEM.
WE LET YOU GO SO THAT YOU WOULD LEAD US TO GREY.
!!
BUT TO ORDER YOU KILLED...
SEEMS WE BOTH MISJUDGED HIM.

THAT... THAT'S IMPOSSIBLE!
MR. GREY WOULD NEVER DO SUCH A THING!
YOUR WOUNDS ARE QUITE DEEP.
WE'LL DISCUSS THIS LATER.

SHEESH! YOU GUYS ARE PLAYIN' DIRTY. I ALMOST FEEL BAD FOR HER.
WE'RE IN A WAR, KID.
SO RIGHT NOW, THE ENDS JUSTIFY THE MEANS.
OR DID YOU FORGET ABOUT MILLENEAR?
HEY. BACK ALREADY?
THAT'S SOME LOOK...
...BERYUN.

WELL? HOW'D IT GO?
I DON'T KNOW. SHE'S EXTREMELY SHAKEN.
HMM... I DAMN WELL HOPE SHE FELL FOR IT.
WE NEED TO KNOW WHERE GREY TOOK MILLENEAR.
HOW WAS DESH?
HE PULL IT OFF?
I THINK SO.
I STILL SAY...
...YOU GUYS...
...ARE PLAYING DIRTY.

...UH...

HMM...

WELL, LOOK WHO'S UP.
I'D LIE STILL. DON'T WANNA OPEN UP THAT WOUND.
GREY...
...WHAT...
I WAS ONLY TRYING TO RETURN...
...TO GIVE MY REPORT.
WHAT DID I DO?
I SERVED HIM FAITHFULLY.
I TRULY RESPECTED HIM.

AND THIS...
...IS HOW MY LOYALTY IS REPAID.
DAMN HIM.
61
I WILL GUIDE YOU...
I'LL TAKE YOU TO MR. GREY PERSONALLY.
HE AND I HAVE UNFINISHED BUSINESS.

FINE! BUT WE LEAVE NOW!
BERYUN, GET ALL THE GEAR TOGETHER.
REMI AND EIJI, WAIT HERE WITH THE OLD MAN.
WAIT.
YOU'RE NOT GOING ANYWHERE.
WHAT DID YOU SAY?
IF YOU ATTACK GREY NOW, YOU'LL DIE. YOU DON'T HAVE THE SKILLS.
TRAIN WITH ME FOR THE TOURNAMENT, RUDBICH!
I CAN'T LET YOU GO UNPREPARED.

I'M GOING, OLD MAN.
DON'T TRY TO STOP ME.
PFFT...DIDN'T THINK YOU'D LISTEN TO REASON.
HYAH!

WRONG MOVE!
착
UNHH?!
팡

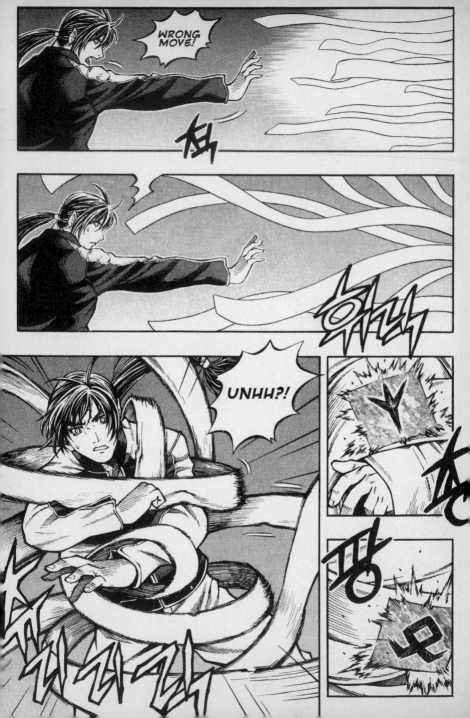

AH!
TSK...
LISTEN TO THE OLD MAN.
DON'T THINK SO. ANCIENT BINDING SPELL.
YOU BASTARD!
RELEASE ME BEFORE I TEAR YOU TO PIECES!!
IF YOU INSIST ON GOING, I WON'T STOP YOU.
BUT HE'S NOT READY.
IF YOU SAY SO.

I DON'T THINK YOU UNDERSTAND HOW DANGEROUS GREY IS.
IF THINGS BEGIN TO GO BADLY...RUN. RUN FOR YOUR LIVES.
I CAN'T STRESS THIS ENOUGH. GREY IS CAPABLE OF NEARLY--
OKAY, I GOT IT!
PLAY NICE, KING TUT!
BE BACK SOON!
BERYUN, STICK CLOSE TO OUR FRIEND.
YOU'LL BRING MILL BACK, RIGHT, RETT?
GOOD LUCK, MASTER!

BECAUSE OF THIS GUY, I BOUGHT FISHNET STOCKINGS FOR THE FIRST TIME.

INABA EIJI

HEIGHT: 170
CM WEIGHT: 64 KG.

I JUST PAINTED HIS HAIR WITH BLACK INK.

I BORROWED THE IDEA THAT HE IS FROM MU-YUN-CHUN-SIN SECT.

HIS OFFICIAL JOB IS AS A NINJA, BUT IN ACTUALITY, HE HAS NO INTEREST IN BEING A NINJA.

INABA EIJI / 19 YEARS OLD / NATIONALITY: JAPAN
WE ORIGINALLY CREATED THIS CHARACTER TO BE A PRETTY BOY FOR THE YOUNG GIRL READERS. BUT HE JUST TURNED OUT TO BE ANOTHER PERVERT LIKE RETT.

I'M INABA EIJI THE 16TH OF THE MU-YUN-CHUN-SIN SECT'S MAGIC PAE-SIN FAMILY.

EIJI IS MORE OF A CHARACTER CREATED FOR VISUALS, INSTEAD OF STORY.

SPECIAL FEATURE: CHARACTER REALIZATION FILE

HANG ON, MILLENEAR. WE'RE COMING!

PHEW-
LUCK BE WITH YOU, WARRIOR.
TO BE CONTINUED IN REBIRTH VOLUME 14!

After the deadline
THE AUTHO
CIRCUMSTA
YOU SAY REBIRTH IS TOO VULGAR?
MY PEN BURNS WITH DESIRE!
WHAT AM I TO DO?!
QUITTING SM
PHYSICAL HE
THESE DAYS
ME
CENSORS!
I DEFY YOU ALL!
THE SALES SUCK ANYWAY! I'LL DRAW WHAT I WANT!
IT'S NOT LIKE I'M DRAWING "BATTLE VIXENS"!
MAJOR STRESS BOMB FROM QUITTING SMOKING

AGE 197 / HEIGHT: 172 / WEIGHT: 48 KG

FOR A PRETTY MINOR CHARACTER, SHE'S A REAL PAIN-IN-THE-ASS TO DRAW.

RANG: A VAMPIRE

ORIGIANALLY, RANG WAS SUPPOSED TO BE KILLED OFF BY DESHWITAT. BUT THE AUTHOR HAS AN UNNATURAL CRUSH ON HIS OWN CREATION, SO HE KEPT HER ALIVE.

SHE'S NOT A PARTICULARLY POWERFUL VAMPIRE, BUT SHE'S A SCRAPPER AND A SURVIVOR.

THIS IS A SEXY WOMAN WHO KNOWS HOW TO USE HER SEXUALITY TO GET WHAT SHE WANTS.

NEED TO DEVELOP NEW EYES...

THE COSTUME WAS INSPIRED BY A CERTAIN GAME SHOW HOSTESS.

BERYUN'S EYE: COLD EYE WITHOUT ANY HIGHLIGHTS.

RANG'S EYE: CAT-LIKE

REMI'S EYE

MILLENEAR'S EYE: STANDARD

The Great Republic of Korea
2002. 6
THANKS FOR READING "REBIRTH"! SEE YA' NEXT TIME!

RED DEVILS
SUPPORTERS CLUB
FORZA
COREA
BE THE Reds!
BE THE Reds!
Seems Woo is a big soccer fan, as well.

Preview: Vol. 14

Having duped Mr. Grey's underling, Rang, into aiding them, Rett and Beryun venture into the would-be Vampire Lord's lair. It is a valiant effort to rescue their captured comrade, Millenear, from an unknown, but certainly ominous, fate. Meanwhile, Deshwitat struggles to free himself from the forced tutelage of Draistail, the eccentric vampire, recently defected from Grey's legions. But even if Deshwitat should manage to make good his escape, will he be in time to help his teammates? Or for that matter, will he even be a match for the formidable Mr. Grey himself?

TOKYOPOP SHOP

VAN VON HUNTER

EVIL NEVER DIES...
BUT EVIL STUFF DOES!

FROM THE
WINNERS OF
TOKYOPOP'S FIRST
RISING STARS OF
MANGA™
COMPETITION

VAN VON HUNTER

EVIL NEVER DIES...
BUT EVIL STUFF DOES!

FROM THE
WINNERS OF
TOKYOPOP'S FIRST
RISING STARS OF
MANGA™
COMPETITION

TOKYOPOP® SHOP
WWW.TOKYOPOP.COM/SHOP
HOT NEWS!
Check out TOKYOPOP.COM/SHOP The world's best collection of manga in English is now available online in one place!
PLANET BLOOD
THE TAROT CAFÉ
SOKORA REFUGEES
WWW.TOKYOPOP.COM/SHOP
0 00000 00000 0
• LOOK FOR SPECIAL OFFERS
• PRE-ORDER UPCOMING RELEASES!
• COMPLETE YOUR COLLECTIONS
Sokora Refugees © Kurt Hassler and TOKYOPOP Inc. Planet Blood © 1996 Kim Tae-Hyung, Daiwon C.I. Inc.
The Tarot Cafe © 2005 Sang Sun Park/ SIGONGSA

HANG ON, MILLENEAR. WE'RE COMING!

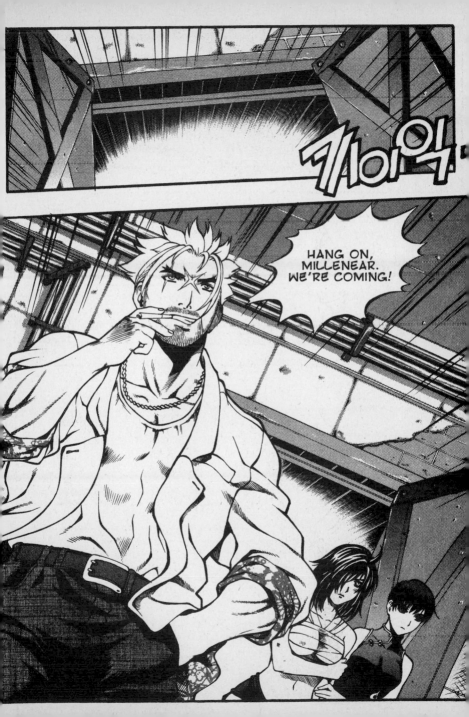

PHEW-
LUCK BE WITH YOU, WARRIOR.
TO BE CONTINUED IN REBIRTH VOLUME 14!

After the deadline
THE AUTHOR'S CIRCUMSTANCES

YOU SAY REBIRTH IS TOO VULGAR?

SO WHAT'S WRONG WITH VULGAR?!

QUITTING SMOKING MAY BE GOOD FOR PHYSICAL HEALTH, BUT I'M REALIZING THESE DAYS THAT IT'S NOT GOOD FOR MENTAL HEALTH.

MY PEN BURNS WITH DESIRE!

WHAT AM I TO DO?!

CENSORS!

I DEFY YOU ALL!

THE SALES SUCK ANYWAY! I'LL DRAW WHAT I WANT!

IT'S NOT LIKE I'M DRAWING "BATTLE VIXENS"!

MAJOR STRESS BOMB FROM QUITTING SMOKING

BECAUSE OF THIS GUY, I BOUGHT FISHNET
STOCKINGS FOR THE FIRST TIME.

INABA EIJI

HEIGHT: 170
CM WEIGHT: 64 KG.

I JUST PAINTED HIS
HAIR WITH BLACK INK.

I BORROWED THE IDEA
THAT HE IS FROM MU-
YUN-CHUN-SIN SECT.

HIS OFFICIAL JOB IS AS A NINJA,
BUT IN ACTUALITY, HE HAS NO
INTEREST IN BEING A NINJA.

INABA EIJI / 19 YEARS OLD /
NATIONALITY: JAPAN
WE ORIGINALLY CREATED THIS
CHARACTER TO BE A PRETTY BOY FOR
THE YOUNG GIRL READERS. BUT HE
JUST TURNED OUT TO BE ANOTHER
PERVERT LIKE RETT.

I'M INABA
EIJI THE 16TH
OF THE MU-
YUN-CHUN-
SIN SECT'S
MAGIC PAE-SIN
FAMILY.

EIJI IS
MORE OF A
CHARACTER
CREATED FOR
VISUALS,
INSTEAD OF
STORY.

SPECIAL FEATURE:
CHARACTER
REALIZATION FILE

AGE 197 / HEIGHT: 172 / WEIGHT: 48 KG

RANG: A VAMPIRE

FOR A PRETTY MINOR CHARACTER, SHE'S A REAL PAIN-IN-THE-ASS TO DRAW.

ORIGIANALLY, RANG WAS SUPPOSED TO BE KILLED OFF BY DESHWITAT. BUT THE AUTHOR HAS AN UNNATURAL CRUSH ON HIS OWN CREATION, SO HE KEPT HER ALIVE.

SHE'S NOT A PARTICULARLY POWERFUL VAMPIRE, BUT SHE'S A SCRAPPER AND A SURVIVOR.

THIS IS A SEXY WOMAN WHO KNOWS HOW TO USE HER SEXUALITY TO GET WHAT SHE WANTS.

NEED TO DEVELOP NEW EYES...

THE COSTUME WAS INSPIRED BY A CERTAIN GAME SHOW HOSTESS.

BERYUN'S EYE: COLD EYE WITHOUT ANY HIGHLIGHTS.

RANG'S EYE: CAT-LIKE

REMI'S EYE

MILLENEAR'S EYE: STANDARD

The Great Republic of Korea
2002. 6
THANKS FOR READING "REBIRTH"! SEE YA' NEXT TIME!

RED DEVILS
SUPPORTERS CLUB
BE THE Reds!
FORZA COREA
BE THE Reds!
BE THE Reds!
Seems Woo is a big soccer fan, as well.

Preview: Vol. 14

Having duped Mr. Grey's underling, Rang, into aiding them, Rett and Beryun venture into the would-be Vampire Lord's lair. It is a valiant effort to rescue their captured comrade, Millenear, from an unknown, but certainly ominous, fate. Meanwhile, Deshwitat struggles to free himself from the forced tutelage of Draistail, the eccentric vampire, recently defected from Grey's legions. But even if Deshwitat should manage to make good his escape, will he be in time to help his teammates? Or for that matter, will he even be a match for the formidable Mr. Grey himself?

IN DREAM WORLD: FOLLOW YOUR DREAMS... BUT BEWARE OF THE NIGHTMARES!

Nightmares are bad enough when you are asleep, but in Dream World, nightmares are real monsters! Drake, Hanee and Kyle battle these night terrors with special "In Dream Cards," magical cards that have unusual and devastating powers. Those who wield the cards gain the power of the elements, and our heroes must master the cards before they are put into a permanent state of sleep!

TOKYOPOP
In Dream World
JAE-HO YOON
This knife of flame!

OT
OLDER TEEN
AGE 16+

For more information visit: **www.TOKYOPOP.com**

EDITORS' PICKS

TOKYOPOP MANGA SUPPLEMENT

Faeries' Landing
You Hyun
1

BY YOU HYUN

FAERIES' LANDING

Following the misadventures of teenager Ryang Jegal and Fanta, a faerie who has fallen from the heavens straight into South Korea, *Faeries' Landing* is both a spoof of modern-day teen romance and a lighthearted fantasy epic. Imagine if Shakespeare's *A Midsummer Night's Dream* had come from the pen of Joss Whedon after about a dozen shots of espresso, and you have an idea of what to expect from You Hyun's funny little farce. Bursting with sharp wit, hip attitude and vibrant art, *Faeries' Landing* is guaranteed to get you giggling.

~Tim Beedle, Editor

Tramps Like Us
Vol. 4
Yayoi Ogawa

BY YAYOI OGAWA

TRAMPS LIKE US

Yayoi Ogawa's *Tramps Like Us*—known as *Kimi wa Pet* in Japan—is the touching and humorous story of Sumire, a woman whose striking looks and drive for success alienate her from her friends and co-workers...until she takes in Momo, a cute homeless boy, as her "pet." As sketchy as the situation sounds, it turns out to be the sanest thing in Sumire's hectic life. In his quiet way, Momo teaches Sumire how to care for another being while also caring for herself...in other words, how to love. And there ain't nothin' wrong with that.

~Carol Fox, Editor

SGT FROG
TOKYOPOP
TWO
MINE YOSHIZAKI

BY MINE YOSHIZAKI

SGT FROG

Sgt. Frog is so absurdly comical, it has me in stitches every time I edit it. Mine Yoshizaki's clever sci-fi spoof showcases the hijinks of Sergeant Keroro, a cuddly looking alien, diabolically determined to oppress our planet! While some E.T.s phone home, this otherworldly menace has your number! Abandoned on Earth, Keroro takes refuge in the Hinata home, whose residents quickly take advantage of his stellar cleaning skills. But between scrubbing, vacuuming and an unhealthy obsession with Gundam models, Keroro still finds time to plot the subjugation of humankind!

~ Paul Morrissey, Editor

TOKYOPOP
Ahmed Hoke
Two

BY AHMED HOKE

@LARGE

Ahmed Hoke's revolutionary hip-hop manga is a groundbreaking graphic novel. While at first glace this series may seem like a dramatic departure from traditional manga styles, on a deeper level one will find a rich, lyrical world full of wildly imaginative characters, intense action and heartfelt human emotions. This is a truly unique manga series that needs to be read by everyone—whether they are fans of hip-hop or not.

~Rob Valois, Editor

고오오오
MetLife
ooo...
빵
빵
빵

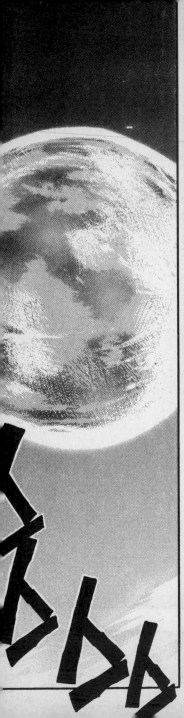

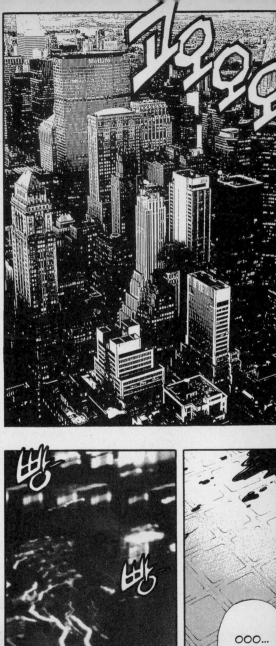

GOOD WORK, EIJI!
UP YOU GO, NOW!!
UH...?
COME TO ME...
...MY HIDDEN FLOWER!
UM... OKAAAY.
ULP.

HEY! SNAP OUT OF IT, LAD!
YOU LET HER ESCAPE WITHOUT SUSPECTING A THING!
JUST LIKE WE PLANNED!
UH-HUH...
ALL RIGHT. FIRST STEP COMPLETE.
I'M SURE BY NOW SHE THINKS SHE'S HOME FREE.
NEVER KNOWING WE'LL BE RIGHT BEHIND HER.
BUT I MUST SAY, EIJI, I'M REALLY IMPRESSED!
GREAT ACTING!
......
......
IT WAS...
...ACTING, RIGHT?
....

NO WORRIES, EIJI!
THE RESULT'S THE SAME!
UM... RIGHT.
IT'S BERYUN. WE'RE READY TO GO.
GOOD.
LET'S HAVE SOME FUN.

HUFF-
HUFF-
HUFF-

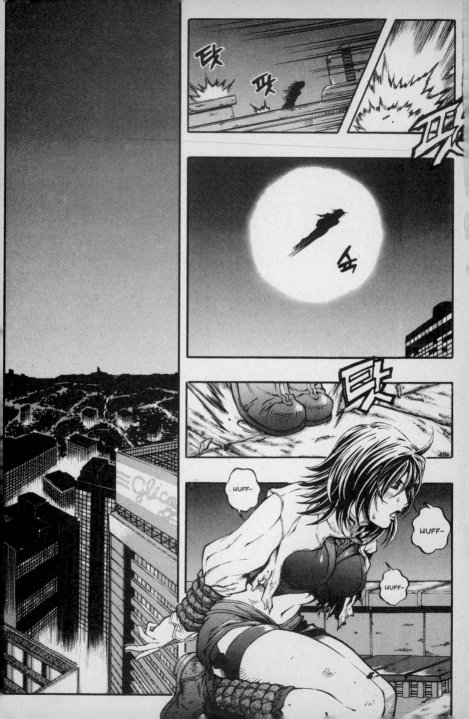

THIS SHOULD BE FAR ENOUGH AWAY.
THESE ROPES. SOME SORT OF SPELL ON THEM. CAN'T GO BACK TO GREY LIKE THIS...
DAMMIT! HAVE THEY FOLLOWED ME?!
EH?!
AAAHH!!

AHH-KAFF!
OOH...
COUGH
COUGH--
UH...AHH...
WHO...
WHO THE
HELL ARE
YOU?!
HUKK!

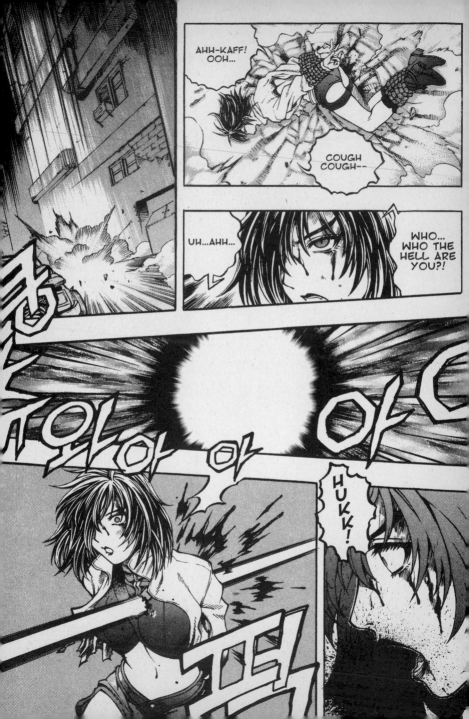

176

After the deadline

THE AUTHOR'S CIRCUMSTANCES

YOU SAY REBIRTH IS TOO VULGAR?
SO WHAT'S WRONG WITH VULGAR?!
QUITTING SMOKING MAY BE GOOD FOR PHYSICAL HEALTH, BUT I'M REALIZING THESE DAYS THAT IT'S NOT GOOD FOR MENTAL HEALTH.
MY PEN BURNS WITH DESIRE!
WHAT AM I TO DO?!
CENSORS!
I DEFY YOU ALL!
THE SALES SUCK ANYWAY! I'LL DRAW WHAT I WANT!
IT'S NOT LIKE I'M DRAWING "BATTLE VIXENS"!
MAJOR STRESS BOMB FROM QUITTING SMOKING

BECAUSE OF THIS GUY, I BOUGHT FISHNET
STOCKINGS FOR THE FIRST TIME.

INABA EIJI

HEIGHT: 170
CM WEIGHT: 64 KG.

I JUST PAINTED HIS
HAIR WITH BLACK INK.

I BORROWED THE IDEA
THAT HE IS FROM MU-
YUN-CHUN-SIN SECT.

HIS OFFICIAL JOB IS AS A NINJA,
BUT IN ACTUALITY, HE HAS NO
INTEREST IN BEING A NINJA.

INABA EIJI / 19 YEARS OLD /
NATIONALITY: JAPAN
WE ORIGINALLY CREATED THIS
CHARACTER TO BE A PRETTY BOY FOR
THE YOUNG GIRL READERS. BUT HE
JUST TURNED OUT TO BE ANOTHER
PERVERT LIKE RETT.

I'M INABA
EIJI THE 18TH
OF THE MU-
YUN-CHUN-
SIN SECT'S
MAGIC PAE-SIN
FAMILY.

EIJI IS
MORE OF A
CHARACTER
CREATED FOR
VISUALS,
INSTEAD OF
STORY.

SPECIAL FEATURE:
CHARACTER
REALIZATION FILE

AGE 197 / HEIGHT: 172 / WEIGHT: 48 KG

RANG: A VAMPIRE

FOR A PRETTY MINOR CHARACTER, SHE'S A REAL PAIN-IN-THE-ASS TO DRAW.

ORIGIANALLY, RANG WAS SUPPOSED TO BE KILLED OFF BY DESHWITAT. BUT THE AUTHOR HAS AN UNNATURAL CRUSH ON HIS OWN CREATION, SO HE KEPT HER ALIVE.

SHE'S NOT A PARTICULARLY POWERFUL VAMPIRE, BUT SHE'S A SCRAPPER AND A SURVIVOR.

THIS IS A SEXY WOMAN WHO KNOWS HOW TO USE HER SEXUALITY TO GET WHAT SHE WANTS.

NEED TO DEVELOP NEW EYES...

THE COSTUME WAS INSPIRED BY A CERTAIN GAME SHOW HOSTESS.

BERYUN'S EYE: COLD EYE WITHOUT ANY HIGHLIGHTS.

RANG'S EYE: CAT-LIKE

REMI'S EYE

MILLENEAR'S EYE: STANDARD

Seems Woo is a big soccer fan, as well.

Preview: Vol. 14

Having duped Mr. Grey's underling, Rang, into aiding them, Rett and Beryun venture into the would-be Vampire Lord's lair. It is a valiant effort to rescue their captured comrade, Millenear, from an unknown, but certainly ominous, fate. Meanwhile, Deshwitat struggles to free himself from the forced tutelage of Draistail, the eccentric vampire, recently defected from Grey's legions. But even if Deshwitat should manage to make good his escape, will he be in time to help his teammates? Or for that matter, will he even be a match for the formidable Mr. Grey himself?

TOKYOPOP SHOP

VAN VON HUNTER

EVIL NEVER DIES...
BUT EVIL STUFF DOES!

FROM THE
WINNERS OF
TOKYOPOP'S FIRST
RISING STARS OF
MANGA™
COMPETITION

SPOTLIGHT TOKYOPOP MANGA SUPPLEMENT

IN DREAM WORLD: FOLLOW YOUR DREAMS... BUT BEWARE OF THE NIGHTMARES!

Nightmares are bad enough when you are asleep, but in Dream World, nightmares are real monsters! Drake, Hanee and Kyle battle these night terrors with special "In Dream Cards," magical cards that have unusual and devastating powers. Those who wield the cards gain the power of the elements, and our heroes must master the cards before they are put into a permanent state of sleep!

TOKYOPOP
In Dream World
1
JAE-HO YOON
This knife of flame!

OT
OLDER TEEN
AGE 16+

For more information visit: **www.TOKYOPOP.com**